October Sequence
(1 - 51)

Sheila E. Murphy

The author is grateful to the publishers of the following publications where sections of this work first appeared:

Otoliths

Anti-Heroin Chic

e ra/ tio

Last Stanza Poetry Journal

TXTOBJX

The Nonconformist Magazine

Cover image by Sheila E. Murphy

isbn ISBN: 978-1-948637-08-4

P.O. Box 342 Roanoke, VA 24003

mOnocle-Lash Anti-Press

monoclelash.wordpress.com monoclelash@gmail.com

1/

Here’s kiss think

Reasoned ivy

Strained as weather

Curved to fathom

Platformed feathers

There to be a flock

First cornered

Then erased as plumes

And wind frayed caveats

Boost the plane

Once crossed acrostic

As a nude once known

Mown down with cinders

Near a large framed

Symphony still flat

As ironed lace

2/

Sandwich something
Make a story posse-lined
With floorboards
Infant pre-long lines
Attracting tap shoes
Slipper styled
In margins pensive
As the sudden dream
That follows stiff lead
Of the habit system
Drawled across
The nonce Novemberly
A rich pose in a poverty
Disguised to be enormous before
Cold then beetled
Out of boredom finding
And inventing drums

3/

Halo in a whisper

Rings quill feat still

Shimmed of chaparral for now

The shoots in foreground wild

Caucasian surface

Impregnable pumpkin white

Absolved of cliched orange

Of defunct previous guy

Tedious with throat rasp

Prattling daybreak through nightfall

Talk show blather

One indeed prefers a clean wide spate

Of peace why not now via

Cordless playthings that guide

The writhe away from this *ici*

4/

Thanks G for “meaningly”
My glee spills over plush oats
In white morning bowl
As I collide with breath
Above the nest and beckon
In good charm time warm
To reach uncut collateral
Free lurching this way
On impulse to betray
Those deserving of betrayal
In silken chestnut cloisters
Near the wind beyond the window
Precious please be pretty now
And ride the damages
To safety at the pinhole hour
Of depth avowed

5/

Keep upkeep lithe skin-deep
Come-hither nurse yet wet
Behind the lobes approaching
Scrum fed parkway’s kismet
Gone to suds against the elbow
Smuttering God help
The dreamed z’s
More disrobable than scansion
Standard issue pawnshop
Short short story
Drizzled onto pagelets winking
Slurry dram shop legal pique
The clean breeze nominates
Syllabic feats new names announce
The well-bred fingerings of classifieds
To match high need versus neanderthal
Meandering in ship shape forest
High beams waiting to stick
The prim routine by taut young
Gymnanzies

6/

Tepid to the tap shoes weighing
Bandy-legged zero-sum grams
Achieve un-touch of midnight morning
Weedy as conformity to breast feed
Syllables disguised as young bad moods
Upon the altar cloth against the sotto
Shades of Otto's grades made cinders
In the wheatfields grazed upon
By dandy lights about to break
Into some butter stains along
The chin line after yogic stances
Held against mimesis of eternity
Until one chime commands cessation
Cheated of a sugar feigning depth
In forest wheeze the light spats
Between branch and silhouettes
Of leaves and stern vibrato

7/

Attention frosts when episodic
And discreetly missing, the hiss
Resentment plocks qua door is
Sealed Lucille you're outta luck
The clover and the loam go
Wide away from reach
Likewise the "tendre croppes" occupy
In situ where contempt resides
Why not lie down alone
And watch the matter weeded from intent
As you convey the jazz within
Minus odometer who cares
The hills are wool the skies
Comply with recitation of a breach
Of silence splayed across dark yards

8/

Uncubicled for now at breakfast
Table the day long nothing
In common with the lifelong friend
Now whittled to Febrezing through
The digital minutiae
Reciting plaintext or staying still
Old plaudits share the scarcity
Of store shelves
Shipping crates in port
And lorries stuck as
Poverty remands delay
And zilch defrays the cost
Of stasis rarely coexisting
With connection the complexion
Pretty dry a window’s open
What is there to see through now

9/

Encore teach me colors
On the plastic clothespins
Pre-spin cycle
Wealth is what we had when
Posture was comprised of back length
Several inches high
I filled little shirts I was
All eyes learning the stylized mauve
And Army olive green
Just talk again so I can tell myself
The daylights we are out of
Will be seen and will prevail
Like wind out of the east
And spare change will resound like preparation
For some seeds to scatter
From the hand that is my own

10/

The Tipperary comatose endowment
Floats about the grain we seed
When cordial as Kissimmee hosts
Our dancing in an empty lot
Framed as the site of shelter
And palatial parity if same
Can be elapsing silence
What you love that you may hear it
Lift above the sensory induction
Flowers become white when tired
Something we can learn is spruce
I have an obligation to enroll
In your tutorial the sluice will hold
Intact if you repay what
You are wilded on a cushy day

11/

Soroptimist declension varies me
To tilt the other limelight
In the way perpetually shading
Glockenspiel and say so gilded
While eruption stains the pillars
With detained imbroglio for now
The nuisance is attractive
And the latitude that complements
The longitude keeps Brailling toward
The see-through walls
Once stalled into their being
Staved as the inevitable
Boulder to be brash against
Threaded vocabulary stirring pilfered
Letterpress and silver fractured blur
Some semitones unleashed from tact

12/

Social pressure media presumes
Subsumes resumes beginning with no
Advantage you may join
If happy accidents half planned
Befall you who expect
The hinges later taken
For granted (“for granite” in
A curious vernacular of eggcorn)
In whatever purview
You may mine not mine
Not yours and shine you
Tell yourself that “popular”
Means you have a name
And in the population you
Both blend and stand out
From the others others are
Your window into you

13/

Corner lot dotted with
Swiss army knives prepped for
A bounty cast like fine sprawled
Nets across the acreage under
Fire under surveillance under
Willow swish above the divan
Rivaling facets of industry as
Acorns roll pre-capture
On film nobody claims nobody
Sees via pseudonymous
Novel sleeves of story panes
Of glass and aspiration
Why not detail detain repay
The diastole from memory unclogged
As winter comes predictably
Unplanned yet known as mown
Sweep of the crop and lawn and fact
Made part of the proceedings
Vast to the beholding eye
Under a broad green shade

14/

Wicked problems blur the mind
Away from clarity the trapdoor
Protecting solvency I mirror
What I reach for stalled
By hesitation to reveal what is
Not necessary to share
And curiosity belongs to others
It is fitting I let go
The string of homonyms
Declensions patched and dwindling
Let’s say paradise has dieted too long
And now attracts too few
Shows zilch interest in
The zero-sum fragility
We number name and quiz
In thrall toward decibels
And hammer pops to make
A window lateral

15/

She’s still
Wise today she is
Alert I ask a few things
And the answer is
Profound I have to sift
To sort and scatter
What to learn from what
She says I know there’s no
Disaster plan who needs
The worst a singing feeling
Sinks into the comfortable
Couch I need a conch to hear
What is beneath her language
Offer me a path and I will
Substitute the faculty
Of sitting where I am
To learn from her what is
Removed from habit systems
In the nearby dark

16/

Go inside and flatten daylight
Let go standing water
And be free of
Insects needing lunch
Remove yourself from status
Of a food group and take part
In the sting the rodeo
The bulls and boys convene
And clash and scatter ashes and applause
How many accidents equal
The thrill in thrall
How many adjectives must be
Heaped upon the Everest of our thinking
Picture diametrically ensconced
In chaos theory chaos actuality
Chaotic breeze apart
From hot springs why not

17/

What do you
Want of me from
Me what do I
Offer what is
Innocence gone stale
Am I an army are we
Joined what is
Our purpose what am I
To do why do you
Keep asking what
You need to know
To know is to cease
Learning the sole sentence
Works then goes away
The highlight lifts from page post
Pagination slow to hear
Yourself hear me
I am the derivation
Of experience belonging
To you longing to be
You and I absolve
Myself of your digression
Search and replace
The winter of our words

18/

Don’t warn me about
Brittlebush the fragrance
Hurts don’t let the ocotillo
Change your magnet heart
Be wild with me awhile
I have been here am not
From here what difference
We are not alike let us ride bikes
Let’s censure predators
Who reproduce like weeds
Let’s not be who they
Show themselves to be
As neighbors shrill their way
Through walls I do not
Want to hear I like a chilly
Metronome prefer host cities
To be hospitable and softly
Far away that I may learn
Myself and you and season
My way forward to familiar
Moments fretted with
Untended melody

19/

Tithe through winter frame
The justice you imagine freehand
Plunks ideas into chairs
Whipstitches small thought posses
Into whittled moments fresh
From Tennessee the woman
I shall meet is elderly she
Carves apart from company
She sells what she produces
Leaving symmetry asymmetry asunder
Fills space with the tonsure
Of indifference and God is harmless
Not imaginary she invents
A juried self to lean on
And accepts the flurry of
Small scars that will evaporate
Some starlit morning
When the darkness has expelled
Its robust absence
In a threadbare stream

20/

Quiet (See: aware)

Calls attention to three women:
Minnie A carving through solitude
Of the pandemic and last night
Another born the same year
Could not appear for a reading of her work
Today I visit the third person
Born that year she is giving it her all
Her health softer her forehead full
Of sensing she no longer has the energy
To want to use it and she cries
I cry neither of us believing
What happens to the body despite
Reading the Dhammapada
Her wisdom and her kindness
Still she watches over me
Asks am I all right
As the whittling woman goes on
Transforming wood to beauty
And their contemporary perhaps
Will soon be well enough to speak

21/

Saints Peter Gerald Mary Douglas Rick and Craig
Reside where there is no path
To find you I believe no path is needed
Same with Helen Thomas Bernadean
Cecilia Bernard prior Thomas Bessie
Now I’m cold as I am with you
Keep you safe knowing you are loved
As winter comes and winter
Holds our coat for us
We sleeve in or sleeve away
Until the warmth returns
I have no anchor I am used to now
I recreate myself I sample
History to locate tendencies or rules
I make a mood last or elapse
The soul is always winter
And the light invented by the snow
Defines the streetlamp
Where more snow falls

22/

We suddenly have in common
This continual passive place
From history in plain sight
Or recondite our chances
Once we see them levitate
They agitate an otherwise
Placid world of our own
Making trips to the hosanna
Lean on prior ritual it is so easy
To defer to past tense as the courts
Appear to do the tiny tidy references
To purported fact taken for truth
In bait and switch until
Most precedent lacks prescience
And the breathing room we thought
We knew we needed now
Goes cold enough to walk away from
Wearing chains assigned
Not realigned against
An altar we once needed

23/

Mare of night stretches across
The mental pasture violating
Peaceful sleep an ampersand
Tipped on its side shoved into
A syndrome of resisting
Stuck in pain where movement is illusory
The harshness splintered splintering away
From wholeness wanted a beginning
Minus softness as respite breezewayed
In a wanted silence versus caustic rage
Driving the mind away from
Inner mild potential for sweet views
First felt across infinity of planting
All the mild yards seeking
Light and rain

24/

The next available relationship
Manager purportedly is poised
To help untangle the mess the customer
Did not make and thus I wait
As other customers wait politely
Or impolitely a facsimile of jazz
Splashes through the speaker phone
Preluding the requisite perky nasal
Upbeat fakery intended to feign
Mutual pleasure in this transactional
Reality for which those allegedly served
Must reserve a day each week to subsidize
Highly profitable ways of batching
Us all to formulate a lavish lifestyle
Foreign to the common person
And the common good

25/

“More concise language would be
Clearer for your reader”
Thanks genius if I need you
I will call (collect) so hold
The past in thrall that won’t
Include me or my monetized
Unmonetized endowment of the shim
Weeds and distrait long avenue
Of perceptivision stalking
Not stupidity but meter rhyme
And crib notes from the attic
Lines of code the father
Figure’s letting go of documents
That showcased the enemy plus
Which side prevailed and more
Important how it all went down
And where it went nobody knows
There are the photographs
One finds when looking for
Another thing mayhap a simple
Moment to burrow into for
The fiction clarity becomes
You have somebody’s number
Never known and never mine

26/

"Your call is very impor'an' to us
Please wait for the next available agen'
Thank you for your patience"
Be advised I have little patience
Especially with you who sent me a form
Saying I had not paid something
I had in fact paid I hold in my hand
Two forms of proof
I am listening while trying not to listen
To a tasteless repetitive sequence of
Would-be music resembling naïve doldrums
Mirroring obedience from the unwilling
I am trying to read a brilliant text
By a soul who continues to make life
Worth living studying absorbing realizing
The writer undoubtedly spoke in consonants
With good percussive strength
I despair at sloppy speech
That fails to punch the "d" sound
At the close of a sentence producing
Hash that sounds like "wannette"
I revere the sturdy boundary sounds
That form a stable platform
At once instructive and confirming amen

27/

Mimesis confines vision
To the narrow range we're taught
I teach myself a riveting endowment
Of peace to make from simplest moment
Of a plant risen to eye height
Where next things can flourish
And the guardrails believed required
Begin to pass away from need
Taking lessons on believing in
Simplicity to locate quiet
To shape into a soul
Where cracks and sadness colonize
A joyful spirit broken while
Mending in transition
Toward a sacramental ease apart
From ritual not needed seeming fanciful
Yet all I've ever known

28/

Outside the skin thin brush
With connectivity the male lead
Comes to own the various ad-libbed
Soft beings poised to fill a role
Yet undescribed so accidental friendship
Mirrors the bark of trees protecting
Inner smoothness destined to become
Tables and chairs or maybe hutches
To house china and more keepsakes
That qualify as playthings
That bloom across the yard appearing empty
Yet reverberating presence cared about
Apart from a caress and you look on
As though you could not matter
You just gravitate to failed propositions
That might include
Even a hint of invitation

29/

What is supposed to be a celebration
Frightens those about to celebrate
A better privacy and quiet
Shelter from the noise of guilt rejection
And revisiting a past that happened
Sans intention togetherness
Does not come cheap it's splintered
And fear hurts the epidermis
While the inner organs not left to themselves
Reveal that nothing can become a flower
Visible along the tracks
Hand made from smithereens
To exacerbate already stinging motion
Of the string section immersed in life tones
Shrill to vibrational blends of earth
And blue above incinerating what
We once knew as praxis for the nonce

30/

Not being wanted propels
The engine of the soul beyond
The stuck place of milquetoast
Lasting long beyond its worth
She would have fought mildly to keep
Now freedom offers a gift
Already cherished at first glance
The gleam of all things possible
And learning to expand
Adventurous potential that leaves
Patterned moments in the dustbin
Where they ought to have been
Pitched before without the years
Of comfort as bland habit
Left things as they were
The soul a little tired kept saying yes
Minus language things went on and failed
To change today a power shifted
What seems real the signals
Following first shock when
She began to see a better pattern
Through the mist

31/

Blemished beings propped up
By charitable others
Slowly elevate themselves
Then spit on former friends
As notches on the ladder once realized
Pose an invitation to release
What reminds these disappointed ones
Of who they have become and
To distract themselves they turn cruel
As if erasing what was done to them
What they have made reveals
Informal daylight that frames
What midnight means in code
Water does not cleanse
And warmth betrays what heart
Requires there is no innocence
In the simplicity of what is made

32/

Outside it is warm enough to wear
A top that weighs an ounce
I trot toward my destination
Young grapefruit look like tennis balls
Affixed to the white painted tree
I look on as in a yearbook photograph
My name positioned in the legend
To the right of featured focal point
Of fact finessed by time alleged
In the vernacular as healer
You in your small room shades slanted
Open allowing light to pour across
Your purple velvet blanket
Confirming solitude until I'm with you
As a permanence we've known a vast
Percentage of my life your crystalline
Blue eye light mirrored by the baby doll
Wearing a pink and white cap
Matching rose and rabbit emblem
Patched on the tiny jacket
As insignia to mean in charge

33/

He crosses the line she crosses herself
Their place is low on elbow room
They transmit signals back to
Selves neither rhythmic nor
Arrhythmic penetrating glances occupy
The mirror sought after the lamp
Relays conflicting stories via
Person number gender place or syntax
Yield a handmade shrine
That endows the room with
Functionality unmet as seasons shift
From universal penance to a wanted peace
A lived experience in the wake of
Known momentum while the dowry breaks
Into a dance replete with kismet minus
Kisses and the softness that would make
A kinder world a hammock of
Their mutual history left out
In the ungainly wind to topple
Saplings that comprise a newer world

34/

Future eclipses present tense live
In her mind glutted with fear she sees him
As she sees no self to fashion senses
Into fuel for reinvention after being
Lodged within the circumstance of
Keeping things smooth ironic
Hammer flattens her virtue and her breath
Her shoulders aching with imaginary pressure
She has made by inclination not by hand
But what she has observed then mimicked
For the duration of her threadbare happiness
At the highest level she could maim
By digging into hurts she wears
Until she cries not knowing how
To reason with her instinct or
To find a different attitude or altitude
To free her mindset from a universe
She's trained to see affording challenges
To comprehend or touch and hold within
The trap of what might be stalled
As she keeps acclimating herself
To suspicions already confirmed

35/

A little bulk of metal jams along the busy
Street loud fumes barge past pastel
Sedans and taut trucks blasting
Toward unknown destinations the obstacles
Fatten frenzy and discard intention
Clear enough to see or see through
In the gray wind across cement
And blacktop painted lines uncoded
As the sprawl sans water
Laminates collective mind to mean
The always frenzied press of damage
Seeking contributions seeking fretless
Poise in music always possible to save
The damsel from undress the daylights
Crystallize the pretense and no time
Has timeless properties the world becomes
An artifice commodities perceived by weight
Inform the colloquial turn of phrase
"Tons of people" suggesting that
We weigh them without counting

36/

He requires so much attention
He points to himself and asks
How he is doing she exasperated
Speaks a sentence equally predictable
He keeps inquiring she responds
With whatever used to work
And may still work it's all she has
And she is all he has
He cannot be made peaceful
Regardless of how much approbation
He still wants to know is everything
All right am I indispensable am I
A genius does the world see how
Imperative I am
Is there more that I can do
And is what I have made so far
The most exceptional ingredient
The universe has known am I
Imperative and what's more
How would you describe the importance
Of my being known to be eternal

37/

I am vata you are pitta welcome
To my vegetables my dairy my permitted spice
You cannot consume nuts of any kind we find
An intersection of our tendencies
We do not label compromise we find
A higher path we heal each other
Neither at a time the scriptures
Have been synthesized my seams
Are showing do you know from movies
What that means let's order room service
Let's watch reruns of Forensic Files let's
Hope that law enforcement professionals
Can do their jobs and retrofit
The pavement and the rooftops
To include the many ones we love
Let's serve them food let's plan
A getaway to what remains within us
We are practiced in a Labrador mentality
It's good to glide and to decide
The ampersand is shining golden
Evermore

38/

Amenities derive from statutory innocence methinks
You might be hampered before knowing
The embrace of walls can comfort
Just as kicking up your heels may vitiate
The inclinations of the dour among us
Profiting from incessant statis
Mongrel traits immune to beauty
Tamping even shutters that allow in light
Alongside wind and chasten dabbling
Hitched to aspirations as the rain shine
Rinses tendency to under-simplify where yeast
Allows to rise our stream of breeze
In seeking and exploring how the windows
Tapped lead into homonyms as priestly
Acts of speculation winter mimes
Approach the shore and faces
Blurred by distance come to form
A lottery of patience fortified
As change leads to amorphous depths

39/

Animation gives me hives he said
I’m tired of looking at round shoulders
In blue costumes unfit for human attire
The drawl of portly little footsteps
Soft beyond intention I would rather
View a realistic patch of daylight
With some grit and heavy on the pedal
Toward real life plenty of sharp edges
To smooth the too smooth corner free pretense
As if small beings mindlessly
Invest in comfort for themselves for others
To the detriment of any purpose
Give me a saw to carve the places
Needing sharpness clarity and definition
Give me change to aggravate the hemisphere
To make it grow something beyond
The petty pretty flowers in favor of
A well-earned purity for the duration

40/

Autumn frames a middle way
Preserves the leaf between
Two leaves of wax paper distant
From the tree approaching readiness
For earth viewed as red rust
Nostalgia embedded in stray souls
Leeching comfort from one moment
To live for the smell of a hot iron
Pressing preservation into
The delicate flesh of each leaf
Bringing savor time to match
The golden tinge to warm
The soul drawn in to the unreal
To find truth amid the blessed countenance
As rain lifts even tea dust
From the translation of impulse
To long-term pulse

41/

I see future tense through the stained windshield

As ice taps glass we find momentum slyly

Escape speaks my name to match

A chant more flight than anchor

The world keeps being world

And tires grip surface salt

Desire for quiet leads to magic or its echo

I am always reaching for oases

The sun keeps surface warm enough

For safety solitude and reverie

The cloud light maybe dressing up the plaintext

Of real life as I discover it and lift away

From the long stretch of flat line

I know I should be grateful for

Pathways to a sparkling diary with footsteps

Retrieved then reimagined seeding random

Moves ahead disguised or rendered in principio

42/

A high caliber Magnificat recalls
The reasons for indulgent joy
No puritanical amendment costs the weather
Now and at the burgeoning awareness
That our lives hold still-
Ness nesting last in line
The moment we see frost as
A warm lake star shine warming
Each ingredient as separation
From clear and factual material raised
As in a game with game face
Pointed at opponentry
How many widgets are extracted
From the textbooks of indifference
And mighty jars replete with
What is wanted and the dross of it
Alongside routine prayer symphonic
Weeds and silver next to turquoise
On the arm of someone beautiful

43/

Come slumber near me
Pink the fabric to show see saw
Seem nimble (Oh that label overused as if
Muscular endowment mattered more than depth)
Hypothesize what will matter
More than spring or lockstep or indifference
An overture resplends toward open avenues
You’re still young enough to miss
What you will know as you lose
Recollection once the factual celebration
Has been realized
The yield salt waters doorsteps
One after the next symphonic overload
Chalices your single act embracing
How the windows frame what will have mattered
Needing only a specific noticing
Absorbing and continuing the way
Cadenzas do when light falls soft
Or sharply shapely on the person
Just about to be performing
What weighs more than sprawls
Across the many lifetimes

44/

As fingers leave the sleeves
And reach for clear points of desire
The water rinses foreheads then
The one appointed takes up blessing
As a hobbyist pursuit
And all the faces rinsed act on
The blessing and begin resembling
New life according to the speaker
Quite the bon vivant who names
Names speaks to practices the wilderness
Can hold and leave and straighten
To appear as human made monstrosities
While willows and sweet branches
Elevate beyond conceit of each
Thought center's focus on one's centeredness
As if only commerce equaled
Redemption meaning the sole
Point of being becomes
Be fruitful and multiply

45/

Suddenly everyone is named Jill
Within the mist of captioned call outs
Viable enough to branch into a coma
Littered by expected commas
Dizzying pre-pause a chemical reality
Fosters the foundation seen unseen
As factions qualify against primary sources
Leaning toward advancement brought by wholeness
Then and only then affordances prevail
Amid the use of language of refractive
Smiles pronouncing research questions
That blend and bland the intermediate
Critical friend within shared online space
In contrast to emerging SPACs
Collectively updating valuable tools
You might have missed intended
To free a host of wholesale patterns

46/

Voila the tree the see saw bloat
The sand piped into vortices
Challenged before now venturing
Frame-ward toward the soap box
Peppered with dried minestrone
As though there were no field
Asparagus along the roadside sprouts routinely
Feeding mouths that mouth so little otherwise
And live out days the color gob smack
And the color blue filled with
Cherishable moments that recede
Before the bounty shows itself
And warms us as we drive ourselves
Toward needing less attention
And envisioning us all together as we meet
Infractions along the rural cushions
Littered with permission slips
Encouraging parents to resign design deter
By way of dream their robust children
From becoming larger than
The only context they have known so far

47/

Tell me when to advance that I may pass
The salary the celery the salt
Just as convention therapy allows
Things to occur
Within this artifice
As a quotient held in abeyance
Crashes roundly soundly
Toward fracture
As a blimp that meets shrill cacti
On the limbic field
Where dawdling prevails and intellect
Discouraged ventures home
Its tail between its legs
The pegs and pedagogy
Rifled with the undue murk
Of syllables within the silos
We erase from an army
Of consoling principles

48/

Are we abstract enough to clean
From our pure skin the guilt of fame
The niche market of bleach the rudder
That draws forth experience for now
We’ll weigh something later
Teach the faculty the facility
To froth the line drawn in a sprint across
The lifeline correspondence course
Correction or collection priorities conflate
The pressure of a prayer for
Social cognitive practices
Buckets of laughter bushels of brine
Portion control made haptic
In a winsome fluid mood ringed
By contentment paltry when lumens
Alight on free-range pastiches
Reflective of luster
In a seasoned thatch

49/

The word “Palmer” a traditional Chicago hotel
A mode of penmanship
A once perky woman
Who advanced beyond her capability
By way of an aggressive stance
Of ladder action and behavior
Common sense necessitates urgent
Strategy reflecting unvalued often
Private shared urge just to write
What each is thinking
Are the training wheels a covenant
Are ashes just for Wednesdays
Is punctuation still dispersed
We must hold conversations hostage
Or in high esteem
To relegate performance to its rightful
Hinge always pertinent to
Relationships sustained

50/

Give me the syrup not the sap
Beyond the stirrups of our ride
Like a leaf a figment or a pause
An option cost the future
Of scraped data
Means and ways to parse
Build spreadsheets for specific
Manipulations to verify the accuracy
Of ten words selected to become
The language *de rigeur* determining
High five-able boot camp life
Consistently reliably beyond
Content provider status
Of the publishers purportedly making available
Direct funds for leading
Scholarship and communication

51/

Cohesion density veers center left
Why don't you just move out
Of the neighborhood having failed
To analyze the network of low centralization
Unfleshed out this graph reveals
Apparent subject matter factual
Connective tissue ignore the direction
Of the arrows serenity's a plus
A quiet place apace why not
Restrict the oval patterns
Quasi matrix longevity the next two
Events will serve as caveats
To curb the place the date
And key words otherwise
A pattern of community of precision
Any precis or bloodline
Carried across the field
Held tentative and shrouded by
A kindled commerce free contusion
Brash with fault lines

Sheila E. Murphy is the recipient of the Gertrude Stein Award for her book *Letters to Unfinished J.* (Green Integer Press, 2003). Murphy's book titled *Reporting Live from You Know Where* (2018) won the Hay(na)Ku Poetry Book Prize Competition from Meritage Press (U.S.A.) and xPress(ed) (Finland). In 2020, Luna Bisonte Prods released *Golden Milk.* Broken Sleep Books brought out the book *As If To Tempt the Diatonic Marvel from the Ivory* (2018). Murphy has authored 44 previous books of poetry. Initially educated in instrumental and vocal music, she is associated with music in poetry. Murphy earns her living as a management consultant and researcher and holds the Ph.D. degree. She has lived in Phoenix, Arizona throughout her adult life.

Her Wikipedia page can be found at:

https://en.wikipedia.org/wiki/Sheila_Murphy

www.ingramcontent.com/pod-product-compliance
Lightning Source LLC
Chambersburg PA
CBHW061255040426
42444CB00010B/2389
* 9 7 8 1 9 4 8 6 3 7 0 8 4 *